18 Reasons Why Mothers Hate Their Babies

A Philosophy of Childhood

Stephen J. Costello, Ph.D.

Eloquent Books
New York, New York

Eloquent Books
An imprint of AEG Publishing Group
845 Third Avenue, 6th Floor - 6016
New York, NY 10022
www.eloquentbooks.com

ISBN 978-1-60860-687-0

Printed in the United States of America

Book Design: Linda W. Rigsbee

This book is dedicated to Darren Cleary,
with deep love and abiding affection and admiration.

"The joys of parents are secret; and so are their griefs, and fears: they cannot utter the one; nor they will not utter the other. Children sweeten labours; but they make misfortunes more bitter: they increase the cares of life: but they mitigate the remembrance of death".

La Rochefoucauld

"Think of the depressing contrast between the radiant intelligence of a healthy child and the feeble intellectual powers of the average adult".

Sigmund Freud

"Children begin by loving their parents. As they grow older they judge them. Sometimes they forgive them".

Oscar Wilde

"There is frequently more to be learned from the unexpected questions of a child than the discourses of men".

John Locke

TABLE OF CONTENTS

ACKNOWLEDGEMENTS

I would like to thank my parents, Val and Johnny, for their constant encouragement, enquiries, support and interest throughout all my writings. My profuse gratitude goes to you both.

Another profound debt of gratitude goes to Darren Cleary, who was the first person to see the potential in this book. He not only painstakingly read this work twice in manuscript form but he also made superb suggestions, subtle refinements, as well as some extremely helpful and constructive comments, all of which were included in the final draft. Darren, I thank you from the bottom of my heart for your deep and fruitful friendship over more than a decade. I dedicate this book to you in love, respect and gratitude. You mean the world to me.

To John Rice, another of my closest friends, who has given me superb encouragement since school-days; thank you John for your stalwart support, untiring enthusiasm and generous time.

Emma Philbin Bowman has been a huge help during all the stages of this book and offered her time generously, especially with editing. Her brightness, creativity and playfulness were of massive and magnificent support to me and without whom this book would be all the poorer.

To Aedamar Kirrane who, likewise, has been of inestimable value in her constant support, endless encouragement, high spirits and energy.

I also extend my gratitude to other close friends for their concern, love, support and interest over the years, especially Thomas and Natalia O'Connor, Helen and Garrett Sheehan, Oisín Breathnach, Abdullah Shalchi, Emil Ahlén, Hugh Cummins, Mészaros Istvan, Fr. John Harris, O.P., Terence Hartley and Fr. Paul Andrews, S.J.

My thanks, too, to all my former colleagues in the Association for Psychoanalysis and Psychotherapy in Ireland, as well as to my students, who have paid to teach me.

PREFACE

T his book is about babies and mothers, but also about fathers, adolescents, lovers and others. It's about need, desire, demand, sex, speech, love, jealousy, betrayal, hardship and hate. It's about a child's universe and families, especially mothers, who struggle to survive.

The context in which I explore the concepts in the book is philosophico-psychoanalytical, but it is written for the layperson as much as for the analyst and educator, the psychologist and philosopher, and all technical terms (which crop up occasionally) are explained. The themes I explore are: the birth trauma; the 'mirror stage' (between 6-18 months); Oedipal drama (between 3 and 5 years); the importance of playing; the child's 'transitional object' (such as the cloth or teddy bear); acting-out behaviour and the difficult child; the only child; the identical twin; the adolescent as someone who doesn't want to be understood; and it outlines the "eighteen reasons why mothers hate their babies", as adumbrated by Donald Winnicott (1896-1971), the renowned British paediatrician turned child psychoanalyst, and which provides a spring-board for my own reflections on the subject.

This is a book of borrowings, snippets, samplings, signposts, fragments, proverbs, maxims, lapidary phrases, axioms, adages and aphorisms. It is a laundry list that can be simply tasted or chewed over.

My main objective has been this one: to aim to alleviate the awful anxiety and guilt that mothers feel when, from time to time, they hate their babies, even as they love them, to tell them that this is perfectly normal and understandable and to explain why this is the case. Whatever else it is, parenting is not child's play.

There is a venerable tradition of aphoristic writing in philosophy, such as I attempt here: Epictetus, Bacon, Montaigne, La Rochefoucauld, Pascal, Schopenhauer, Nietzsche, Simone Weil, Wittgenstein, and in psychoanalysis, too, with the work of Adam Phillips, the child psychotherapist. In theology, too, there have been works of aphorisms by Hans Urs von Balthasar (*The Grain of Wheat*) and Henri de Lubac, S.J. (*Paradoxes of Faith*). And though I don't presume to join these giants in thought, I do try, by citing them, to justify my style and to place it against a certain philosophical, psychoanalytic and theological backdrop.

The ideas in this book owe their inspiration to the work of three great thinkers in particular: Sigmund Freud (d. 1939), first and foremost, the founding father of psychoanalysis, Jacques Lacan (d. 1981), one of his foremost interpreters and hugely original creator himself, and D. W. Winnicott (d. 1971), whom I have already mentioned, who wisely observed: "It is not possible to be original except on a basis of tradition". This book bears that adage out. I also cite a few philosophers, *en passant*.

This is a short-cut, you could say, but if the reader wants to learn more, he or she is encouraged to turn to the texts of the above theorists themselves for further illumination on this intriguing subject. I have included some suggested further reading at the end of this book.

This work is really on the philosophy and psychoanalysis of childhood. In fact, childhood is only 400 years old. In one way or another, it concerns us all therefore, for we have all been children. As Paul Ricoeur, the 20th century French philosopher, noted: "Man is the only being who is subject to his childhood. He is that being whose childhood constantly draws him backwards"[1], while Jean-Jacques Rousseau, the 18th century French philosopher, acknowledged that though he was born a man, he remained a child. But while preaching the importance of good parenting it is said that he put all his five children into an orphanage where most of them died.

A book on childhood is, of course, of interest only to adults. Pascal said a child is not a man. No, but a man is like a child, in so far as he, too, has desire and helplessness and suffers from both of these. Much of our childhood was, as Adam Phillips puts it, "the experience of our parents"[2]. And that is why childhood is

---

[1] Paul Ricoeur, *The Conflict of Interpretations*. Continuum, London and New York, 1989, p. 110.

[2] Adam Phillips, *Equals*. Faber and Faber, London, p. 153.

traumatic. The *innocence* of childhood? The *happiness* of childhood? Those happy few! (Does innocence make us happy?). For Freud, "happiness is something entirely subjective". As Phillips, again, observes: "what could be more traumatic ... than a happy childhood?"[3] What indeed? It is possible to have had a too happy childhood. Possible but unlikely. After all, babies spend a lot of the time crying.

All parents may love their children, be they happy or otherwise. The difficulty, however, is in liking and living with one's children daily[4]. But children have the same problem. We must try both to love and hate them – this is known, in psychoanalysis, as 'ambivalence'. Hate is not always bad. It is a passion, after all. Ambivalence is an achievement to aim for, it seems to me. Essentially, this book is on the 'good enough mother', as Winnicott calls her, and her baby whom she loves even as she hates him/her.

G. K. Chesterton once remarked that children like fairytales unbowdlerised, with the villains killed rather than forgiven, because children are innocent and prefer justice, while adults are guilty and prefer mercy. In what follows I aim for the unbowdlerised truth.

---

[3] Ibid.. p. 154.
[4] See ibid., p. 220.

Aphorisms

Why Mothers Hate Their Babies

It is important that the mother hates, as much as she loves, her child. Hate, after all, is a passion. In fact, the mother hates her infant from the word go. If he or she is not hated, if what is horrible and unacceptable about him is not acknowledged, then his love and loveableness will not feel real to him. This involves "hating appropriately" (D. W. Winnicott). When I am loving somebody I am all the time destroying and mutilating them in unconscious fantasy ("each man kills the thing he loves" – Oscar Wilde). Love kills desire just as fantasy sustains it.

Winnicott suggests that the mother hates the baby before the baby hates the mother, and before the baby knows the mother hates him. First, the mother has primitive love for the child, then hate in response to its demands and ruthlessness. These evoke the hatred of the mother.

There are 18 good reasons why the mother hates her infant: they are all a response to his ruthless use of her. The 'ordinary devoted mother' is full of hate for her child – hopefully. Aggression, at the beginning of love, is a sign of love – all love has a destructive quality. Aggression is part and parcel of the infant's natural appetite. He doesn't mean to hurt or destroy. He *carelessly* loves his mother just as she carefully loves and hates him.

18 Reasons Why Mothers Hate Their Babies
(according to Winnicott, with my comments in square brackets).

1) "The baby is not her own mental conception" [in other words, she didn't magically produce him omnipotently – it involved the father too].

2) "The baby is not the one of childhood play, father's child, brother's child, etc" [in other words, she can't hand it back; it's hers and doesn't seem to play as idyllically as the children she witnessed in other families, her own included, when seen through rose-coloured spectacles].

3) "The baby is not magically produced" [in other words, the stork doesn't bring him or her; it is the result of hard physical labour].

4) "The baby is a danger to her body in pregnancy and at birth" [birth may be the baby's first death as it dies to intrauterine life but the baby's birth is also a considerable risk to the mother].

5) "The baby is an interference with her private life, a challenge to pre-occupation" [in other words, a constant presence that prevents too much drinking, having fun, socialising, going to late night parties, staying out all night etc.].

6) "To a greater or lesser extent a mother feels that her own mother demands a baby, so that her baby is produced to placate her mother" [so grandmothers beware!].

7) "The baby hurts her nipples even by suckling, which is at first a chewing activity" [he hurts her out of love for her, a love understandably not appreciated by mother in pain].

8) "He is ruthless, treats her as scum, an unpaid servant, a slave" ["mommy, give me…"; "mommy do this and that and everything in fact, while you're at it"].

9) "She has to love him, excretions and all, at any rate at the beginning, till he has doubts about himself" [she is called to love him throughout even as he vomits, pisses and shits – "he's a shit"].

10) "He tries to hurt her, periodically bites her, all in love" [and she must endure his attacks, patiently though at times she wants to throttle him – then feels guilt].

11) "He shows disillusionment about her" [he's not impressed; neither is she and she must disillusion him also; he takes her for granted].

12) "His excited love is cupboard love, so that having got what he wants he throws her away like orange peel" [when the cupboard is bare she is discarded, flippantly, and feels empty, let down, depleted, used].

13) "The baby at first must dominate, he must be protected from coincidences, life must unfold at the baby's rate and all this needs his mother's continuous and detailed study. For instance, she must not be anxious when holding him, etc" [he sets the pace, does what he wants, when he wants and she is not supposed to show any anxiety or anger].

14) "At first he does not know at all what she does or what she sacrifices for him. Especially he cannot allow for her hate" [he not only does not know how much she does for him, he forgets it all, doesn't thank her and can't tolerate or permit or handle her understandable hate].

15) "He is suspicious, refuses her good food, and makes her doubt herself, but eats well with his aunt" [or uncle].

16) "After an awful morning with him she goes out, and he smiles at a stranger, who says, "Isn't he so sweet?" [and the mother smiles in rage!].

17) "If she fails him at the start she knows he will pay her out for ever" [that is to say, pay her back forever. It's a no win situation for mother].

18) "He excites her but frustrates – she mustn't eat him or trade in sex with him" [she could "just eat him up" ('cannibal fusionalism') but she is forbidden to engage with him sexually].

The Baby's Birth

Birth is the baby's first death. Every birth is traumatic. It is the first experience of anxiety. Being weaned from the breast (or the bottle, which is a metaphor for the breast) is the second. The breast is the first object of desire. Loss marks and mars the child from the very beginning of life. We can never return to the breast. Each stage in the child's development involves a (fear of) breakdown, a negotiation and a re-adaptation. It is a fact that this attempt can never be wholly adequate. Woody Allen: "I didn't want to be born. I fought it. They had to come in and get me". The minute we're born we begin to die.

A Baby's Baptism

A baby's baptism is when the baby enters into a new birth and becomes a child of God, a new creature. Baptism is the sacrament of faith and by it all sins are forgiven though their consequences remain, according to Church teaching.

"Let the little children alone, and do not stop them coming to me; for it is to such as these that the kingdom of heaven belongs" (Matthew 19: 14-15).

Thus, the adult needs to emulate the child in his open loving, relaxed abandonment, helpless faith, trust and humility.

Here is a selection of quotations from the Bible on the subject of babies and mothers. It amounts to a theology of infancy and motherhood.

Deutoronomy 1: 29-32:   "Yahwey carried you,
                         as a man carries his child,
                         all along the road you travelled".

Psalm 8: 1-2:   "Above the heavens is your majesty
                         chanted by the mouths of children,
                         babes in arms".

Psalm 22: 9-11:   "You drew me out of the womb,
                         you entrusted me to my mother's
                         breasts; placed me on your lap
                         from my birth, from my mother's
                         womb you have been my God".

Psalm 71: 6:   "I have relied on you since I was
                         born, you have been my portion
                         from my mother's womb".

Psalm 139: 13:   "It was you who created my inmost
                        self, and put me together in my
                        mother's womb".

Psalm 139: 15:   "You know me through and
                        through, from having watched my
                        bones take shape when I was being
                        formed in secret, knitted together
                        in the limbo of the womb".

Isaiah 49: 1-6:   "Yahweh called me before I was
                        born, from my mother's womb he
                        pronounced my name".

Henri de Lubac, S.J: "The spirit of childhood is a marvellous grace, and it should be forever repeated with the Gospel that the Kingdom of Heaven is for children and for those who resemble them"[5].

---

[5] Henri de Lubac, *Paradoxes of Faith*. Ignatius Press, San Francisco, 1987 [1948], p. 19.

There is No Such Thing as a Baby

"There is no such thing as a baby, only a baby and its mother" (Winnicott). The two are so totally entwined in the first few months so that there is a fusion and even confusion. Separation happens slowly and begins when the baby starts to see its body as separate from mother.

Why Mothers Should Not Be Too Good...

There is only one thing worse than a really bad mother and that's a mother who's too good. Such a mother constantly ministers to her child, picks him up the minute he cries, (s)mothers him with her love and molly-coddles him, so much so that the 'love' will become stagnant, suffocating and symbiotic. Such a love stifles desire. There are cannibalistic fantasies of devouring and being devoured by mother. If the lack of a mother causes problems, so also does the lack of a lack. One can suffocate in the maternal embrace. The mother ministers to her infant and brings him those objects which satisfy his needs, gifts of the mother's love. Her very presence is token of her love, her absence experienced as the most traumatic rejection. However, too much presence causes anxiety. The optimal model is the 'good enough mother' (Winnicott) and good enough mothering. Mothers must aim, so, not to be good but to be *good enough*. This goes for lovers and friends too.

What is a Father For?

The mother has to disillusion her child. That's her job, as well as to care for, cuddle and caress the child (but not too sexually). The father's 'function' (his job as it were) is to castrate, deprive and lay down the law. In other words, he has to say 'no'. The father is a metaphor. He may or may not be a man. Better to speak about the "name-of-the-father" (Lacan). The name-of-the-father (*le nom/non du père*) stands for the first authoritative 'no', for the first social imperative of renunciation. The father's task is to prohibit, to break the bind that ties mother to child – the dyadic relationship – and to stop it from becoming too incestuous, but not too soon and certainly not too late either. His role is to puncture and rupture the autistic bind tying mother to child, to intervene in that blessed union and to impose a distance between mother and child, for her sake, for his sake and for the sake of the child too.

It is better to have a strict father than a nice father. A nice father may be a friend but is a failure as a father. The father protects and prohibits. His is the voice of the law and authority. The absence of the name-of-the-father is a factor in psychopathology. All fathers are lacking. *Pater semper incertus est* ('the father is always uncertain'): there is always a question about paternity, whereas the mother is *certissima*. The father is perceived of as ideal or as "the father who has fucked the kid up" (Lacan). The father *occupies* the mother. The real father is the spermatozoon; he is the one who is said to be the biological father. It seems we are going from Dad to worse!

On Being Born Too Soon

All human babies are born prematurely, even when they are not. By contrast with animals, the human baby can't walk or talk and is completely dependent on the people around him, for everything really. Everything is undeveloped, marked by discord. The infant is incomplete and lacking; he is totally helpless. We are born too soon. This is evidenced in our prolonged dependency on mother and in our motor incapacity and bodily unco-ordination. The infant's helplessness contrasts with mother's omnipotence. Mother is the first big Other for the child and the first love object. She is an engulfing force. The child must detach from mother in order to enter the social world. There is a connection between well being (*bien être*) and being born well (*bien n'âitre*) – having a good birth experience. The mother provides a 'holding environment' and acts as a 'container' for her child.

Treating Everyone Differently

Every child in a family is different from every other and, therefore, should be treated differently. The mother must not be consistent with her children though sometimes she must be seen to be thus. Consistency is stubbornness; "it is the last refuge of the unimaginative" (Wilde). That said, childhood is conformist, as Jean-Paul Sartre said. One baby, on the other hand, is every baby. Putting it another way: every baby is all babies. It's only after a while that differences between babies become 'apparent' – excuse the pun.

Narcissistic and Perverse Babies

All children are "polymorphously perverse" (Freud), completely egocentric and greedy. The child is a narcissist. That is their charm. Freud speaks of "His Majesty, the Baby". Children compensate for their insecurity and frailty with fantasies of power and omnipotence and that is why, as Freud claimed, every child is a megalomaniac.

Baby Criminals

To some extent, all babies are born criminals. Freud: "The charm of a child lies to a great extent in his narcissism, his self-contentment and inaccessibility, just as does the charm of certain animals which seem not to concern themselves about us, such as cats and large beasts of prey. Indeed, even great criminals ... compel our interest by the[ir] narcissistic consistency"[6]. And, so, these three: children, cats and criminals.

---

[6] Sigmund Freud, 'On Narcissism: An Introduction' (1914), *On Metaps-ychology*. Penguin Books, London, vol. 11, p. 83.

Sexual Children

Children are sexual creatures. Even young children flirt and seduce and provoke and evoke. Needless to say, this does not mean that they can be used, abused or exploited – ever.

The Baby in the World

The world is a "big booming buzzing confusion", in William James's phrase, for the baby. It is absolutely Other for the child; he has to accommodate himself to it. The world doesn't let any of its members be themselves. Compromise is always called for. The family is the first *cell* of society. It is also "the privileged place for the cultivation of neurosis" (Lacan). Families may mess us up but a family is better than a borstal, a prison or an institution. The child must find his own desire even at the expense of his parents.

Demanding Love

The baby's cry is the first demand. All speech is demand. We are all looking for a response. Every demand is for love – "thou love me". The baby has needs. Needs are purely physiological but behind the baby's need for food is the demand, insatiable as it is, as all demands are, for love. Desire is the beyond of demand. All we do is demand. And most of the time, the demand can wait. Don't be in too much of a rush to pick up a crying baby.

Your young son or daughter is in the kitchen as you're preparing the dinner. He or she says, "Can I have some ice-cream? Can I have some cake?" Or "can I have some chocolate?" You might give in to his demands but didn't you notice that once he is satisfied, he demands even more by asking for something else? What your child is really searching for is not ice-cream, cake or chocolate. He is not looking for an actual object but for an object that doesn't exist, for something he will not and can't be given. Of course, he will continue to demand, to try your patience and go on asking for things until he succeeds in finding something that you will not give him. The object of demand does not exist. Loving is being in a state of demand, of wanting to give what you cannot give and to get what cannot be given to you.

Love often involves us placing impossible demands on our lovers. Frustrated demand is the parent of desire. So it is better not to give in to all your child's demands, to everything he asks for or else he will never discover his desire. In order to discover your desire (what you really want), you must experience your demands being unmet. A spoilt child spells disaster. 'No' (the voice of prohibition and law) must be spoken, preferably by the 'father', who, as I said earlier, doesn't have to be a man.

Desire in a Baby's Name

The mother feeds her child words as well as food. Words have an erotic affect especially when they represent the other person's desire. Desire dominates us. What we all desire is recognition. We desire what we lack. Love is wanting to be known. There is a difference between our mother calling us by name and our lovers calling us by name. "All love is love of a name" (Lacan); this means it is important whom you name your child after. Words carry desire. Were you named after your grandmother, uncle, grandfather, nobody?

Desire is trans-generational. In this respect, verbal abuse is worse than physical abuse. Beware of your words used to insult your child, to put him down and to belittle him. Words can, at every moment, touch and profoundly affect living flesh.

Longing for Something that Doesn't Exist

The problem is once we attain the object of our desire (and 'fixation' is the term used to designate a strong attachment to an object/person of desire), we are still not satisfied (thankfully). Desire is metonymical, which means it is always endlessly deferred onto other objects (persons) of desire. Our mothers and lovers cannot fulfil us or make us happy. One person may be substituted for every other. Love is longing for something that doesn't exist. When you love children and animals too much, you love them instead of adults (Sartre).

Parental love and procreation is narcissistic through and through. It is also childish. You want to see yourself born again, anew.

Different Desires

Desire is desire for difference. For example, the teenage son says to his parents, who want him to be a lawyer: "I'm going to be an actor". He's going to be what they don't want him to be. Moreover, the parents' frustrated desires can be heaped onto their children so that a father who became an accountant but who secretly harboured a wish to be a song-writer or singer, forces his utterly talentless son to take up singing lessons.

Serious Play

Playing is what the child takes very seriously. Playing is a way of finding out, through pleasure, what interests you. Playing is the opposite to reality (or maybe boredom) but not the opposite to work. Playing fosters curiosity and inquisitiveness as well as bewilderment. Parents may need to mediate and establish fair play but play is seldom fair. Playing is one way the child comes to terms with his anxieties and children's anxieties, as Sartre remarked, are always metaphysical.

The child who has been slapped by mother now slaps the doll, then cuddles it. Torturing the cat, though, is much more pathological. Bed-wetting, stealing and truancy from school are signals of distress, calls for help. They are positive SOS's. Playing is the child's attempt to work through discord or upset. The child's symptoms are attempts to master anxiety too. A symptom is not an illness but a sign of hope. The child longs to be understood. We all suffer from self-knowledge. Playing well can leave the child satisfied – just like a good dream. Play can involve damaging and restoring objects such as teddy-bears. It is a work of destruction and reparation. But the child may be too anxious to play, to let go. The ability to lose or absorb oneself in play is the ability to let go, to wean. The parent should not invade the child's universe but let him play or read. The child's play should be lively, aggressive and competitive. With mutual play, the child learns empathy for others and concern. The capacity to play is a sign of mental health. But don't ask the child what he is doing when he is playing. Playing is a most intimate and private drama. Leave children to it.

A child's play and a child's pictures possess meaning and can be interpreted. The child's play is like poetic creation. The child at play creates a world of his own. Play is the attempt to master unpleasant experiences. The child will do in play what has been done to him in reality. Children love to play at making themselves disappear. Play is serious. If the child can play and enjoy it there is not much wrong with him even if he wets the bed, throws temper tantrums or stammers. Anxiety is always present in a child's play, hopefully. An adult speaks; a child plays.

On Penises

The baby girl envies the father's or her brother's penis and admires it. She also fears it will destroy her. The boy looks at his sister or mother and fears that he will lose his penis. The castration threat – "stop doing that or I'll tell your father" – issues from mother but usually with reference to the word of the father. The boy sees it is possible not to have a penis. Both the girl and the boy are afraid. But it is better for the parents to be loved than to be feared. Naturally.

The Baby's Bit of Blanket

Most babies have a 'transitional object' from 4 to 6 months of age – a bit of blanket, an old cloth, a teddy bear. It is the first possession, the first 'not-me' object. It is an intermediate area between what is subjectively and objectively perceived. It stands for the breast. Mothers know all about these 'transitional objects'. Winnicott lists *seven* special qualities in the infant's relationship to such transitional objects.

1) "The infant assumes rights over the object.
2) The object is affectionately cuddled and loved as well as mutilated.
3) The object must never change, unless changed by the infant.
4) It must survive being loved and hated and perhaps being the object of pure aggression.
5) It must seem to the infant to give warmth and to move – to show in some way that it has a reality of its own.
6) From the adult's point of view, the transitional object comes from without but not from the baby's point of view; it is not a hallucination.
7) Its fate is to be gradually de-cathected [let go of], so that, after time, it is not so much forgotten or mourned but relegated to limbo; it loses meaning".

So the transitional object is not the actual cloth or teddy-bear the baby uses. It is not the object used so much as the use the baby makes of the object. It is what it symbolises. There is a positive value in destructiveness.

Peek-Aboo

Everybody is isolated, unknown and non-communicative. We want to reveal ourselves while simultaneously we want to keep concealed; we want to play and hide. That is why hide-and-seek is such a popular game ... with adults. Similarly, we take children to films and fun parks in order to amuse ourselves.

Trying to be Desired

The first six months are distressing for the baby. After 6 months, weaning takes place and 'the mirror stage'. Weaning is a psychic trauma. It leaves in the human psyche a permanent trace of the biological relationship it interrupts. A lot depends on how the infant deals with this weaning for it will affect him throughout all his life. The baby is born with needs. To speak is to redeem oneself. The infant also has desires – he wants to be desired by the mother. He attempts to become the object of desire for the mother (i.e., the 'phallus', as a symbol of plenitude and power). A third party must enter this dual relationship. This is the 'name-of-the-father'- it stands for "no!" The infant wishes to be the exclusive desire of the mother; he wants to become her 'phallus' (a "monument erected in the place of lack": Lacan), to plug up her desire; but the mother has other desires that include but surpass the infant – she desires somebody else.

Maternal care is essential for mental health just as maternal deprivation can be the cause of a host of problems. Moreover, a parent may be there physically but not psychologically and may be there psychologically but not physically. For instance, the father may be actually dead but very much present in the child's universe in that the photographs around the house of him and the mother's recurrent recourse to his name act as constant references to and reminders of the father. Contrariwise, a father may be physically present but psychically absent – just 'not there' for the child as he hides himself behind his newspapers and simply opts out of parenthood. "I'll be there in a minute" and never is.

It is possible to have been loved too much as a child. That was Sartre's problem. Hence, as he said: "I loathe my childhood and all that remains of it". Just as it is possible to have had a too happy childhood. Happiness may, in fact, be decided by the age of five!

The 'Mirror Stage': A Time of Jubilation

The mirror stage occurs between 6 and 18 months. It is a formative event in the life of an infant. It happens when the infant is confronted with his image in the mirror. The mirror serves as a metaphor – it may be an actual mirror or a mirroring Other, like the mother. At this stage, the infant is still in a state of motor incapacity and bodily fragmentation but when it looks into the mirror, at some point between 6 and 18 months, it will recognise himself in it and show signs of "triumphant jubilation" (Lacan). The baby sees himself in the mirror as united and is delighted with himself. It is a moment of self-recognition, an 'ah ha' moment of epiphany. Though the infant is still in pieces he perceives himself in the mirror as whole. So the reflection in the mirror is and is not him. The baby is not that image but thinks it is. All through our lives we carry unconscious images of who we are and think we should be which cause us anxiety. These images stem from the mirror stage of development. But I am not my image; I am somebody else, but who?

Being Oedipus

The 'Oedipus complex' occurs between 3 and 5 years of age. It is constitutive of our very being in that we all want to 'marry' the parent of the opposite sex and 'murder' the parent of the same sex as ourselves, unconsciously and *symbolically*. All families are incestuous by definition. There are family romances and alignments. The Oedipus complex consists of an unconscious set of loving and hostile desires that are directed towards the parents and from the parents to the children. "Mummy, when I grow up I'm going to marry you". The father is a rival. The Oedipus complex is triadic. Jealousy is ubiquitous; it is the archetypal sentiment and triadic in structure (envy, by contrast, is dyadic). We can never fully master the Oedipus complex; all we can do is to resolve it partially. Perhaps that's why most people have a problem with authority.

Not Much Happening

School age: from 5 to 12. It is also the 'latency period' (where not much happens). (Woody Allen: "I never had a latency period"). The Oedipus complex is partially dissolved and things settle down before they erupt again in adolescence. The child is learning to separate from mother, to engage in mutual play, to sacrifice his egocentricity, to inhibit aggression, to play without rows erupting, to think systematically, and to enjoy the company of other children. The 'detached dignity' of a 5 or 6 year old signifies a readiness for school. 'Sublimation' occurs (sexuality is channelled and finds a socially acceptable outlet). The child adapts to reality and his or her relationship with parents is more secure; it is also less idealised, which prepares the way for the devaluation that will occur during adolescence. The parents' prohibitions and prescriptions are accepted, and Oedipal desires are surrendered. This latency period is also a time of industry. The child wants to work and produce things; their curiosity and interest in other people are widening and developing, but fears and phobias can increase too. That said, psychically, nothing much is happening.

Incomprehensible Adolescence

The first thing parents need to know about the adolescent is that he does not want to be understood. Understand that and you will have understood him. You can persecute somebody by understanding them.

Adolescence is characterised by a volatile mix of dependency and defiance. Oedipal dramas are revisited and renewed. What is the cure for adolescence and its crises? – the passage of time and the 'maturation process'. Adolescence is a time of drastic disruption, of loss and gain, grief and mourning. The adolescent is incomprehensible and inconsistent, has rapid mood changes and unpredictable outbursts. *You don't have to understand him.* But it's also a time of renewed possibilities; it is a crucial stage in psychological development as he re-experiences the first five years all over again. Early adolescence is concerned with the impact of puberty and new bodily processes. There is a quest for autonomy and a disengagement from parents. "Leave me alone".

The impact of adolescence on the family is great. The adolescent's burgeoning sexuality and growing independence meets with resistances and counter-responses from his family. His or her new body shape is both exciting and disconcerting; the adolescent is concerned with how he looks.

Adolescence is also marked by urgent and compulsive masturbation, which is a way of discharging tension. Fantasies about life are enjoyed and endured and friendships become crucial testing grounds. Intense single-sex relationships are forged and consolidated. The transition: from asexual childhood to same sex groups to hetero- or homosexual pairings. The adolescent is not sure who he is; he feels lonely and misunderstood. It's just as well he does. His uncertainty and insecurity can lead to a defensive distancing, denial, and intellectualisation. Some will flounder as the escapist trend is evidenced in drug and alcohol abuse, in stealing and truancy and in sexual promiscuity. Such a revolt and recklessness can leave the adolescent despairing, hopeless and helpless. Boarding-school is always an option.

Four in Every Bed

We are called to love and to work – the power of *Eros* and the compulsion of *Ananke* (Necessity). For this we are made. One has to establish oneself economically and for the vast majority this entails obtaining a job, marrying, buying a house and raising children. The young adult must leave the child in the past as a lingering memory but retain child-like qualities such as imagination, curiosity, and the capacity to lose oneself in play. Responsibility and obligations are permanently present and a constriction of freedom. We all have a multiplicity of roles – father, mother, lover, teacher, lawyer etc. Identity is not fixed but fluid, not static but in process. In relation to love, it would be wise to experiment and to pair off with different partners safely. The institution of monogamous marriage is not universal and is relatively recent historically. It is a public event that testifies to a private relationship based on economics, the laws of progeny and love and hate.

■

Though we may be monogamous in fact, we are all polygamous in fantasy. It may take two to tango but it takes at least four to make love. There are always at least four in every bed – there's you, your partner, what's going on in your unconscious and what's going on in theirs.

Failing to Learn

Parents vow that next time round they will do things differently, that things will be better with the next child. But experience is not didactic. People do not learn from their mistakes – fortunately. "Experience is a name people give to their mistakes" (Wilde).

What Motherhood Awakens

Motherhood happens quickly. Maybe there is an envy of motherhood in men. The mother was a baby once – it would do well if the mother did not forget this. Every mother has an idealised picture of how it all ought to be – the picture seldom matches up to the reality. Mothers can never win – it's a case of mother, Madonna, whore. Motherhood awakens in the new mother feelings she once had towards her own mother. She needs to let the child know that she has other interests outside her infant. Later, in adolescence, which is a day of judgement for mothers, the mother will attempt to recapture her youth in her daughter. Rewards always come indirectly for mother. The mother is seldom thanked. Motherhood is one mastery that women have over men. We have nothing to match it.

More on Fathers

Every father must be in his 'function' (place/role) as father. There are submissive fathers, battered fathers, blind fathers, bankrupt fathers. There are even good-enough fathers! All of them must occupy the paternal position and actually *be* a father – not a friend. Slapping a child is not physical abuse.

The father must let the child know that he, the father, has a claim on mother's attentions. "I have my rights as well". Everybody, in fact, has a lack and that's why we're so happy. The father's role is to stop the mother filling herself up with her child. If the father fails his child, he or she will look to others to 'castrate' them, to deprive them, to lay down the law. Every child is looking for a way out of the mother's desire. The father should subtly undermine the mother. The real father is the one talked about by mother in his absence.

We can never be certain who our fathers are. By contrast, we all know who our mothers are. That is why fatherhood is a gift in a way motherhood isn't.

A Second Adolescence

When the mother and father reach their mid-thirties to late-forties they become aware of their own life span, of the time they have got to live. There is an inner clock that ticks away and announces that the meridian has been reached. The signs of middle-age are everywhere: the body slows down, wrinkles and grey hair appear, one's earlier self-image alters irrevocably. At this stage, the father and mother will frequently envy as well as appreciate and admire their children or teenagers and their beautiful youth. Mid-life is naturally depressive and one is plunged into mourning. There can be a frantic clinging on to former ways of being and behaving. It's a time of crisis but can be a moment of great unfolding. "Life begins at 40", Simone de Beauvoir said, but by the time she recovered from the shock she had reached fifty!

Insight and change always come through the severest shocks. Mid-life is a metamorphosis, a transformation and transition. It's a time of second adolescence.

Becoming Old

Old age begins at 65 in the USA but a lot depends on intra-psychic factors. This means that one can become old at fifty or thirty. One's children move away and one's friends die. There is the loss of occupation and the status and prestige that go with that. One now has grandchildren and not just children and a little baby addresses you as 'grand-dad' or 'nana'. Tell them to call you by your proper name.

Old age pensioners: what an awful expression. There is more to old age than receiving a pension. What about wisdom?

Old age is the final depressive position in our 'being towards death'. Freud speaks of 'the tragedy of ageing'. Life is composed of stages of crises. Regression (a defensive operation) occurs, which is a universal phenomenon. There is a preoccupation with food and bowel movements. A retreat into the comfort of the past can occur. "This [Ireland] is no country for old men. The young in one another's arms, those dying generations" (W. B. Yeats). But is anywhere? Youth flees old age and beauty too. One never sees oneself as old. One is only old to others. "Other people were my old age," Sartre remarked at seventy-five.

Dreading Dying

Death is not an event in life. It happens outside it. Death is as important as birth. Death is life's closure, the end and impossibility of all further possibilities. Death gives life meaning. To live is to die. Sleep itself, like orgasm, is a little death and love too. Death is not an end – it is a goal. One can typically chart *five* stages when one hears one is going to die, according to Elisabeth Kübler-Ross: 1) denial, 2) anger (rage at the "dying of the light"), 3) bargaining, 4) depression, 5) acceptance.

These stages are not linear or logical. What about the bereaved? They are in a state of acute distress and shock. They feel numb and unable to cope; there can be outbursts of rage or guilt. They seek their lost loved one – they see or sense them everywhere. There is the dread of abandonment, of being left alone and cut off from life's very source. There is primal dread and anxiety. One must hold the memory within and allow the mourning to take place, to accept the fact that they are no longer living, that one will never meet them again. The first year must be survived. But the loss will always be there. There is no cure for that. Except death. Life is a scenic detour, a dance into the arms of death. Nobody can look directly at death. When Sartre died, Simone de Beauvoir remarked that there would be no communication between his ashes and hers. Just so.

Adults fear death just as children fear the dark. Sartre: "All children are mirrors of death".

The Lies of Childhood

Child abuse is a violation of the child's so-called rights (if rights exist at all, for anybody). But some children have fantasies of being seduced. Girls are less truthful than boys, and one should be wary of believing everything they say. The lies of childhood possess great significance. But children do not lie without a reason. In 'Two Lies Told by Children' (1913), Freud suggests that the lies of children are often a response to the lies of adults.

Incest is always a shared secret and conspiracy. Sexual abuse is shrouded in secrecy. Child sexual abuse is a power problem. Children are often not believed (or too believed). There is the permanent fear and risk of retaliation and retribution at disclosure. The silence of the incest years can be met with a deafening silence following disclosure as well. When they look back 'victims' are often more annoyed over not being believed than angry at the actual abuser. There are 'fixated' abusers and 'regressed' offenders. In essence, incest is a misuse of power; it is not motivated by sexual desire, as such.

Day-Dreaming to Reality

We are poor if we are 'normal'. Only through daydreams and illusions can the infant get to, what people like to call, 'reality'.

Mothering Melancholy

The mother continually gives birth to her infant. The mother's depression (for example, post-natal depression) can sabotage the child's development. The child has to deal with the mother's mood; this is difficult. The child can't use his mother's depression to escape from his own. The lively child tries to make it up to his mother for something he hasn't done and can't quite understand.

The Child as Truth

The child is the moment of truth for the mother.

Sexual Streams

The baby goes through three phases, three libidinal stages: the oral, anal and phallic ones. These three phases correspond with three erotogenic zones: the breast, the anus, and the clitoris/ vagina or penis. At the oral stage (breast feeding) everything is put into the mouth and enjoyed there. In the anal stage, where the child is being toilet trained, the child is learning bodily mastery, how to hold onto and let go of faeces. In the phallic phase, the child is enjoying his or her own body sexually. He may play on his penile organ in phallic *jouissance* (he has the title deeds already in his pocket – Lacan). These are the three rivulets in the child's psychosexual development. Let's hope he paddles rather than drowns in the streams of his sexuality.

Four Moments in Childhood

Four moments: there is the primal scene (the parents copulating); there is intrauterine life and the birth trauma; there is seduction (the fantasy of seduction and the emergence of sexuality); and there is castration (the castration complex – the fear that because the girl has no penis, she was castrated).

Speaking of fears, the baby fears falling apart. The mother's job is to provide a 'facilitating environment' for the baby –a primary maternal preoccupation. The mother's function is to be an auxiliary ego to the infant. She stops him from being overwhelmed by impingements. The baby has an illusion of omnipotence but then comes into contact with reality. The ego is a bodily ego – think of Michelangelo's statue of David. We are embodied beings. The anorectic child has a poor self (ego/body) image. The anorexic "eats the nothing" (Lacan).

The mother must fail her child adequately. Only when she fails does the baby learn to cope. The failing can't be too severe or premature, though. The mother's act is always a hard one to follow.

Ruthless Babies

In the early stages the baby experiences no concern. It is ruthless/rootless. The baby destroys what it gets excited about. It is tempting to regard newly born babies as playthings or pet monkeys – out of revenge.

Gifted Children

There are gifted children. Many of them are obnoxious. Yet genius/giftedness is having the courage and conviction of one's talents, and courage is always original. For Wilde, beauty was a form of genius as it needed no explanation.

Deserving Parents

Children get the parents they deserve (Sartre).

What Mothers Know

Only mothers can tell us anything about infants. Nobody else really knows anything, especially psychologists.

What Aristotle Knew

There is no such thing as sentimentality in mothers. Their love is as real as their hate. Mother love is the prototype of all love. Aristotle had adduced this centuries ago.

The Baby as a Going Concern

The baby is always a 'going concern' for mother. Speaking of money, every child is a little capitalist.

We only stop being children (on going concerns) on the death of our parents.

The Baby's Knowledge

The baby knows about mother better than mother knows him or her, until he or she is born, that is. Mothers love their children more than fathers do, for they love them as products of their own being. Childless marriages may last less long than marriages where there are children. Sadly, children can stitch their parents together. If there are no children, sometimes pets are purchased as substitutes. Unlike humans, dogs don't mistake you for anybody else. But like humans, they come when they are called – eventually.

A Philosophy of Childhood 69

Discovering Desire

The child's task is to make good the failure of his parents. When somebody says, "You are your father's son," the only response is, "No, I am my own person". The child is always trying to discover what the desire of the parents' is, what their position is towards desire. In order to become a separate and unique human subject the child must 'murder' his parents and find his own desire. Parents, for their part, must take care not to hold on to the love of their children by making them depend on their help, or by buying their love or by keeping them in a state of infantilism.

A Child's First Things

The child's first words need to be *heard*, hearkened to, just as the adult's first memory and first dream tell a tale too.

Faeces are the child's first gift, just as his crying is his first demand. The child's shit is offered for the sake of someone he loves (Freud).

Complaining Parents

When parents complain about their children, in effect they are complaining about themselves. And when adults talk about their childhood or their parents they are never talking about their real childhood or their real parents.

Intrusions

Imagine this: a younger brother is born. The older child reacts to this intrusion in his life, to this radical upset and confusion by bedwetting, soiling and stammering, or by attacking his actual sibling. In this way, the child expresses his hostility and jealousy towards his detested sibling. He might kill a teddy-bear who symbolises, in fantasy, the brother who has arrived to take his place. He may express his anger in other ways too – he may refuse to eat. All siblings are usurpers.

Without Reproach

If a child is behaving dangerously and violently towards his younger brother or sister the mother should *talk* to the child (not argue), putting his grievances into words but without condemnation and without reproach. That said, the right word is hard to come by. Sometimes, the mother is required to be her child's analyst.

It's impossible to lie to one's mother.

When Adults Lie to Children

Myths about storks bringing babies don't damage children. What damages and disturbs children is the deception of adults who frequently lie to children and who assume an air of talking truthfully when they're lying. The result of an adult lying to a child is to call a halt to the child's curiosity and to block him from further intellectual incursions.

Being Afraid

Children develop phobias because they're afraid of something (and desire it): the phobia is a symbolic substitute for what gives them anxiety. The cause of anxiety is the lack of a lack, i.e., too much (mothering) presence.

On Transitivism

'Transitivism' refers to a type of identification and is often observed in the behaviour of small children. For example, a child hits another child of the same age on the left side of his face and then feels the right side of his own face [inversion] and cries out in feigned pain. Don't be taken in by this.

Babies, Mothers, Symptoms

A baby is a symptom for mother. Just as woman is a symptom for man.

Who is in Whom?

There is the child in the family but there is also the family in the child. One is always talking to (and having sex with) more than one person at a time.

Aiming to Disappoint

The mother should enjoy being annoyed with the baby when it cries. The baby is worth coming to know, isn't he? The mother must be *alive* for the child and aim to disappoint him frequently.

At the Breast

Breast-feeding is a veritable orgy of pleasure, for both parties, even when it's painful.

Four Kinds of Crying

There are *four* kinds of crying, according to Winnicott: crying out of satisfaction, pain, rage or grief. Mothers know all this anyway. But Mum's the word! (They know but in a way it is incommunicable). The baby is, thus, exercising his lungs, signalling his distress, expressing his anger or else producing a song of sadness.

Ludwig Wittgenstein: "Anyone who listens to a child's crying with understanding will know that psychic forces, terrible forces, sleep within it, different from anything commonly assumed. Profound rage and pain and lust for destruction"[7].

---

[7] Ludwig Wittgenstein, *Culture and Value*. Blackwell Publishing, London, 2002 [1977], p. 4e.

What Babies Do

Babies change mothers. Do they change fathers? A father is only born when a child is. But the child is father to the man (Wordsworth).

Ambivalence

Children idealise then hate their parents. Only later will they see them aright, that is to say, as people who are worthy of both hate and love. Ambivalence is the best one can hope for.

What Mothers Can't Do

A mother can't make a child happy. If she gives in to his demands and lets him have his way, then she certainly won't be happy and nor will he.

Who We Want

Nearly everything is set in stone before the age of five, including sexual orientation. Everyone carries within them a bisexual disposition. Heterosexuality is not natural – it is normative.

"Childhood decides everything" (Sartre).

Racist Children

Every child is a racist due to his acknowledgment of difference.

'Normal' Children?

There is no such thing as a 'normal' child or a 'normal' mother. Mothers and children are neurotic, that is, if they are not psychotic or perverse. We have three 'choices': neurosis, psychosis or perversion and all three are decided before and around the time of the Oedipus complex.

Burdens and Baggage

All children are burdens, just as all parents are baggage.

Only One

Being an only child has several drawbacks: he has no play-mates; he will never experience the arrival on the scene of a younger brother or sister; he will never observe his mother's pregnancy; or see her bathing or breast-feeding another child. These are valuable experiences he misses out on. He can't find experiences and expressions for his hatred. The only child is selfish and is used to demanding too much. All siblings dream of being an only child.

Same Difference

People speak of 'identical' twins. In these cases it is difficult for mothers to meet two infants' immediate demands simultaneously. The mother of so-called identical twins will be trying to find out how they are different from the moment of birth. It is important to know one thing: identical twins are *not* identical; if they were they would be the *same*. They are similar but not the same. So take care not to dress them the same. Isn't it bad enough that they look the same?

The Child Who Steals

What of the child who steals? He is not a thief. There are at least thieving tendencies in every child. It is not theft if he goes to the fridge and takes some cheese or the cupboard and takes some sweets. He is not looking for the object (the sweets, for example) but what the object represents. He is looking for mother but doesn't know this. If he steals sugar, unconsciously, he is searching for his mother's sweetness for this is what the sugar symbolises. The mother is the person from whom he feels he can take things. Stealing is an expression of a desire for more love. It is something positive.

The Absence of Shyness

The so-called 'normal' child is shy and nervous in the presence of strangers. The absence of such shyness may be an indication that something's wrong with the child.

There is a time when every baby should cry when it's picked up by a stranger.

Teaching Sex

Sex education cannot be taught to children (or to anyone for that matter) but that doesn't and shouldn't stop a school from teaching biology. "Nothing that is worth knowing can be taught" (Wilde).

What Delinquents Seek

What of the anti-social child or the delinquent? The antisocial child is looking outside the family to provide stability and containment for his needs. The 'antisocial tendency' is a reaction to maternal deprivation. The delinquent child is looking for parental authority, though he doesn't know it. In his acting out behaviour, he is searching for a strict father. He offends against society to establish control inside. Aggression is a reaction to frustration and an endless source of energy. It is of course better that a child 'lose' his teddy than that he kill his younger brother or sister. Every loving involves hurting and hating. The child needs to harness these energies in the task of living, that is to say, in the job of loving, hating, playing and working, later on.

Darkness

Children confront us with the shadow of their parents.

Preferably Married

The optimal situation for the child is to be brought up by one mother and one father, by a man and a woman who are preferably married to each other. Adoption is not a right; it is a privilege, as are children.

All Children

All children are painters; to be more precise, they are abstract expressionists.

All children are scientists; to be more precise, they are radical empiricists.

All children are philosophers; they relentlessly ask the basic yet boundary questions. Our aim: "to see the newness that is in every stale thing when we looked at it as children" (Patrick Kavanagh). Philosophers, like children, ask and wonder – relentlessly. The child knows what he is interested in and where to get inspiration from. He is driven by what he doesn't know and cannot understand. The child's innate wonder and curiosity is a form of appetite, his knowledge is derived from sexual curiosity. He clamours for attention; all children are hysterics.

In Every Crêche.....

There are beasts in every crêche just as there is a brat in every child.

Exposure

Children show up your weaknesses and pass on family secrets to strangers.

No Place to Be

The child struggles to survive, to secure a place in the 'symbolic order' of society, to find a place in the world. He will never be successful: once he is weaned, he is permanently psychically homeless. He has no place to be. Every child has something in him that is missing. Their desire is unappeasable. But the child has the capacity, too, for relish and pleasure.

Shutting Them Up

Children want to know about all things sexual and adults shut them up and stifle them by telling them that they should be interested in other things. Like what, for example?

All children are hedonists – they are aesthetes. Sometimes, these aesthetes are beautiful to watch, these "immediate ones", as Kierkegaard, the Danish philosopher, called them.

But there is a cynic, too, in every child.

Silent Speech

Adults teach infants to speak just as infants (*in fans* = without speech) teach adults how to remain silent – all sounds, syllables and silences, signifying what, precisely? Too many words spoken to a child can give the experience of being force-fed.

Terrible Two's

What to make of a terrible two-year-old as he throws a tantrum?: that he is fully alive and absolutely engaged, of course.

A Child's Rage

Rage tells a tale of abandonment, betrayal and the loss of love – and hope. Yes, that too. When we become enraged as adults, we become like children again, but without sympathy.

Blackmailing Parents; Begging Children

All parents are blackmailers just as all children are beggars.

The child, "Please, can I have that. Give it to me".

The parent, "If you tidy your room now and look after your sister later, you can have it".

What Parents Do

Every child feels humiliated because adults make children dependent on them. Parents satisfy a need, then take it away again. And, so, these three: humiliation, shame and rage.

Senescence: Second Try

As adults, childhood is our goal. The aged lose themselves in second childhood. That is why young children and old people get on with each other. Don't they? All the pleasures of adulthood are, at bottom, childhood pleasures (Adam Phillips)

More Than Can be Given

Clarity interests no-one. That's why children exert a fascination upon us. In their babbling they are like psychotics. Neurotics can only envy and be wrong.

We are all children in that we all want more than we can have, more than what can be given to us. A parent, "What do you want?" A child, "Everything". A parent, "When do you want it?" A child, "Now".

When Nothing Matters

Mental health is laid down between the ages of birth and five. Depression is common in children as well as adults. It occurs when *nothing* is the matter. Just as manic activity may be a defence against depression, so can 'dry eyes' be a flight from sadness.

A child often feels he is wrong or wicked. But a child can become depressed out of an unconscious identification with a depressed parent. After all, the child lives within the orbit of his parents' character.

Introduction to Anxiety

Anxiety is a universal phenomenon. The earliest experience of anxiety (apart from birth): being insecurely held as babies.

Alone with Others

We humans are alone, radically so, with others. Winnicott talks about being alone, as children, in the presence of our mothers. But as adults, can we bear being alone in the presence of our lovers? We are called to. All love hurts (love bites). In reality, love is *the* experience of loneliness. It is only when we are alone that we can try to discover for ourselves who we really are — whatever that means.

Childhood and Its Discontents

Childhood and its discontents: its high dramas, dreams, moments of depression and ecstatic jubilation, terrors, tremors and tragedy, high hopes, betrayals, the anxiety of jealousy, petty squabblings, secret discord, grim darknesses, grief, greatness, empty spaces, shudderings, stammerings, silences, dependency, defiance, murderous fantasies, separation, struggles against despair, bodily becoming, resistances, repression, regression, love, hate, play, work and happiness (perhaps).

On Weeping

What child hasn't had reason to weep over his parents? What father has really got to know his son?

The Hidden Child

Younger brothers or sisters are more fortunate than older ones – apart from the bullying, that is. If young men have visions, old men dream dreams. There is a child hidden in every man. Women might want to discover the child in man.

What Man Means

Man is a means for woman – the purpose is the child.

Affinities

Women understand children more than men do, but men are more childish than women.

Reasonable Jealousy

St. Augustine observed a child, who could not yet speak, glaring at his foster brother, sharing his mother's milk – he was pale and had a poisonous stare. Jealousy is born with love. But jealousy is reasonable. Love isn't. Love always places impossible demands on others.

Three Things to Do Before Dying

The baby gives birth to the man and the woman. Hell for woman may be old age, as Nietzsche, the German philosopher, remarked, but is it any better for man? Does anyone know how to be old? *Three* things we hope to do before we die: father/ mother a child, plant a tree, pen a book. For the writer, books are children.

Little Philosophers

Aristotle didn't spend much time teaching his student Alexander syllogisms or geometry; he taught him valour, virtue and greatness of soul. Parents should teach by example. What you learn when you're young will help you in your "white-haired wretchedness" (Montaigne). It would be good for the young to study philosophy, which, unfortunately, is rarely taught in schools. The philosopher Jacques Derrida asked, "who's afraid of philosophy?" In a letter the philosopher Epicurus says, "Let the young not reject philosophy nor the old tire of it". Philosophy can be taught even to three year olds through reading them stories rich in moral symbolism. Philosophy nurtures a careful spirit of enquiry into everything. It helps people *see*.

It is said that children should neither be seen nor heard, but it is good for children that they mix with their parents' friends, with people of all ages and visit foreign countries. But above all, they should be encouraged to question. If they can form or frame a question at all, it is also possible for them to hear the answer (if there is one), no matter what it is.

Car Stickers

'Baby on Board'. What does this really mean on a sticker stuck on the back of a car window? These: "we're happy, fertile hetero-sexuals"; "keep your distance"; "my child is more important than you". The message is drenched in arrogance, triumphalism, paranoia and phobia. The effect it has: to produce unconscious aggressivity in other drivers. So take the sticker off. Why not put a sticker up saying "Mother on Board"?

Elements of Hate

All parents conceal a hatred for other parents' children.

Indebtedness

We owe mothers everything. Isn't every day mother's day?

AFTERWARD

A few of my friends, after having read this book, remarked to me that it contained a certain 'perverse logic'. I hope, dear reader, you will think that the latter outweighed the former.

I hope, too, that you will not think it to have been too outrageous or, worse, unpalatable. I intended to be forthright and to stimulate thought. But also to be truthful. And a bit playful. It is a depth-psychological and philosophical impression.

I took up a hammer, like Nietzsche, who described himself as a 'hammer philosopher'. The reader must judge whether I have managed to hit at least a few nails on the head.

I am a philosopher, trained too in psychoanalysis, who has written a book on children. What, so, is the relation, if any, between children and philosophers? Ludwig Wittgenstein, the 20th century Austrian philosopher, provided an answer to this question and, so, let the last word go to him: "Philosophers are often like little children who first scribble some marks on a piece of paper at random and then ask the grown-up "what's that?""[8]

---

[8] Ludwig Wittgenstein, *Culture and Value*. Blackwell Publishing, 2002 [1977], p. 24 e.

SUGGESTED READING

Sigmund Freud. *On Sexuality*. Penguin Books, vol. 7, 1991.
(A classic work on the subject).

Jacques Lacan. *Écrits: A Selection*. Routledge, 1977.
(Difficult but fascinating).

Adam Phillips. *Winnicott*. Fontana Press, 1988.
(An accessible introduction to the work of Winnicott).

Adam Phillips. *Monogamy*. Faber and Faber, 1996.
(Superb and thought-provoking. I am much indebted to this and other works by Phillips).

Adam Phillips. *The Beast in the Nursery*. Faber and Faber, 1998.
(Again, a fascinating and absorbing read – much recommended).

Adam Phillips. *Equals*. Faber and Faber, 2002.

Donald Winnicott. *Through Paediatrics to Psychoanalysis: Collected Papers*. Karnac Books and the Institute of Psycho-Analysis, 1992.
(This contains the famous list of eighteen reasons why mothers hate their babies and much more besides).

CPSIA information can be obtained at www.ICGtesting.com
Printed in the USA
LVOW082057290911

248441LV00008B/21/P